All About
Barack Obama

Paul Freiberger
& Michael Swaine

BLUE RIVER PRESS

Indianapolis, Indiana

All About Barack Obama
Copyright © 2020 by Paul Freiberger & Michael Swaine

Published by Blue River Press
Indianapolis, Indiana
www.brpressbooks.com

Distributed by Cardinal Publishers Group
A Tom Doherty Company, Inc.
www.cardinalpub.com

ISBN: 978-1-68157-119-5

Cover Design: David Miles
Book Design: Dave Reed
Cover Artist: Jennifer Mujezinovic
Editor: Dani McCormick
Interior Illustrations: John Knapp
Fact checker: Kaitlyn Duling

Printed in the United States of America

10 9 8 7 6 5 4 3 2 1   20 21 22 23 24 25 26 27 28 29

Contents

All About
Barack Obama

Introduction

His full name is Barack Hussein Obama II. His father herded goats in Africa as a teen before becoming interested in the government. His mother was an anthropologist and spent much of her life in Southeast Asia. He had a passion to make the world a better place. Thinking about his unusual background and his unusual name, he once asked if the United States could elect "a skinny kid with a funny name" to be President.

The country said yes, we can.

In 2009, Barack Obama became the 44th President of the United States. He was the country's first African American President. He was the first President who was born in Hawaii. He was the first President from a mixed-race family. He rose from humble beginnings to the most powerful office in the United States.

He is one of the youngest people ever elected President, and has received many awards. In addition to winning the Presidency twice, he was the only President to win the Nobel Peace Prize in his first year in office, he had written two best-selling books before being elected, and he was the first African-American President of *Harvard Law Review*. He graduated from Harvard University with high honors.

On the way to the Presidency, he focused on helping others. He worked as a community organizer, helping to improve neighborhoods. He was a civil rights lawyer, helping to make sure people got fair and equal treatment. And he taught about the United States Constitution in law school.

After his Presidency, he continues to work for communities and to encourage young people to make a difference. He created the Obama Foundation to inspire and empower people to change their world. This book provides an introduction to his life so far.

Chapter 1
Barack's Family

Barack's mother, Ann Dunham, was born in Wichita, Kansas. His father, Barack Obama Sr., was born in Kenya.

To understand Barack Obama. we have to begin by learning about his parents, Barack Obama Sr. and Ann Dunham, and how they met, and the remarkable son they had.

When the father of the future President got off the plane in Honolulu, it was the end of his first trip by airplane. It was the first time he had ever been out of Africa. His name was Barack Hussein Obama Sr. And here he was in Hawaii!

There were beautiful beaches and palm trees. But he had seen all of those things back home in Kenya. He had worked in Nairobi, the capital city of Kenya, and it was just as big and busy as Hawaii's capital, Honolulu. What really impressed him were the faces.

His own face was dark. This was 1959. The civil rights movement was just getting going in the United States. In some parts of the country, African-Americans were told they couldn't go to the same schools as white children, and that they had to ride in the back of the bus. Martin Luther King was leading a fight to get African-Americans the same right to vote as all other Americans.

But Hawaii was different. The faces Barack saw in Honolulu were every color. There were Japanese, Filipino, European, and native Hawaiian faces. And a few African faces like his. Barack's dark skin made him just one more different culture in a place of many cultures.

It was really his personality that made him stand out at the University of Hawaii. That was what he was here for, to go to college, and he fit in right away. He was confident and cheerful and popular, and looked sort of like a professor with his black-rimmed glasses and his pipe. He talked like a professor, too. People would come to listen to his deep and melodious voice when he was lecturing to everyone at George's Inn, or in a campus hangout called the Snack Bar.

He would tell everyone who would listen about his African country of Kenya. Kenya was changing from a British colony to an independent nation, and Barack planned to play a big part in that change. There were no high-quality colleges in Kenya, so some of the best students, like Barack, were sent to study elsewhere. Barack had come halfway around the world to get a college degree so he could go back to Kenya and use his education to help to make life better for everyone in his home country.

He worked hard. He took extra classes so he could finish a four-year program in just three years. He got a job at a coffee shop to help pay for school. But he also went dancing at Stardust Lounge and hung out with friends, listening to music and eating pizza. He had fun.

Barack Obama Sr. earned a Doctorate in Economics from Harvard University.

To Ann Dunham, Hawaii was not fun.

Her parents Stan and Madelyn, also called Toot, had named her Stanley Ann. She didn't mind having a boy's name. She knew who she was. But later on, people called her Ann, her middle name. Ann was born in Kansas but she had lived in many States, because her dad kept moving the family to new places. She finally got to settle down for a while when they lived in Seattle, Washington. She went to high school there and made lasting friendships. But then dad decided it was time to move again. This time they moved across the ocean to Hawaii.

Hawaii was beautiful, but Ann was miserable. She wanted to stay in Seattle. She didn't want to leave her friends. She wanted to go to college at the State university there.

But her father said there was money to be made in Hawaii. Hawaii had just become the 50th State. Ads said, "Come to the newest State!" Airlines had just started jet service to Honolulu. Many people would be visiting and even moving there. They would need a place to live. Stan hoped to make money helping people to buy houses or furniture. Ann could go to college here, he told her.

Barack's grandparents, Stan and Madelyn Dunham, raised him from the age of 10 in Honolulu, Hawaii.

So here she was in Hawaii.

She did love college, though. The University of Hawaii's campus was beautiful, and there were so many different cultures and races. That was the best thing.

Ann was smart and a hard-working student. School had always been easy for her. And she knew what interested her. She loved learning about other countries and cultures. She thought she might become an anthropologist, traveling the world studying other cultures.

Ann and Barack met in Russian class. She wanted to study Russian because it was another culture she didn't know enough about. Her skin was as light as his was dark. They fell in love, got married, and at 7:24 PM August 4, 1961, their one and only child was born, a little boy they named Barack after his dad.

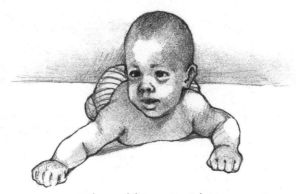

Baby and future President.

But they didn't have much time together as a family. Both Ann and Barack Senior were full-time students. They were really focused on their classes and their career plans. Ann traveled to Seattle, and Barack Senior finished his degree and flew away again, this time to Harvard University in Massachusetts for graduate school. He was going to study economics. He was sticking to his plan to return to Kenya and improve conditions for people there. Ann didn't think she and little Barack fit into those plans.

Ann did manage to get back to Seattle for one year, studying anthropology at the university there. But she and little Barack moved back to Hawaii after a year. Ann needed her mom and dad to babysit little Barack while she was in class. She moved in with them.

Babysitting was tricky because Ann's parents, Madelyn and Stan, were both working. Madelyn worked in a bank and Stan worked in a furniture store.

But Stan found time for little Barack. He took him to the beach. He bought him his first shaved ice. One of the first astronauts to fly into space came through town and was in a parade. Stan took Barack and lifted him up on his shoulders so he could see over the crowd.

Sometimes Stan took Barack to work with him at the furniture store. Customers would laugh when the saw the little boy grinning and giggling as he bounced on the beds.

Soon Barack was old enough for kindergarten. Ann and her parents were all there to take him to school on that first day. He loved Miss Kazuko Sakai's class, with its rainbow of skin colors. His teacher said he was a little shy, but a very happy little boy, with a twinkle in his eye.

Grandfather Stan often took Barack to the beach while his mom studied.

And then suddenly, they were moving to Indonesia.

Chapter 2
Indonesia

After divorcing Barry's father, Ann married Lolo Soetoro, another foreign student at the University of Hawaii. Lolo was from Indonesia, a country in Southeast Asia. Lolo, like Barry's father, wanted to take his American education back to his home country to help people. Barry thought Lolo was fun. In Hawaiian, Lolo means crazy. Lolo thought that was funny.

Barack was nine years older than his sister Maya,
here with their mother, Ann Dunham with her second husband,
Indonesian businessman, Lolo Soetoro.

When Lolo finished his degree, he had to return to Indonesia. Ann stayed in Hawaii to finish her degree, and then she and Barry flew to Jakarta, Indonesia, to live with Lolo.

Indonesia is a country of over 17,000 islands and many volcanoes. Its motto is "unity in diversity." Its people are Muslim, Hindu, Buddhist, Christian, and have skin of many different shades.

The plane landed on Indonesia's largest island, Java, and Barry and Ann found themselves in its capital, Jakarta, with its millions of people. Barry held onto Ann's hand as they left the airplane. The sun was beating down and it was hot and noisy. Lolo met them and drove them to their new home.

Barry saw many three-wheeled motorbikes in the streets of Jakarta. Jakarta had more bikes and motorbikes than cars. He saw a ten-story tall monument topped by a sculpture of the Hindu monkey god Hanuman, with a man's body and an ape's head.

They were to live farther out, in one of the poorer areas. The countryside they passed through had been through war and was still torn up.

They drove past swamps on either side of the main road. In their neighborhood, houses were closely packed. The street their house was on was dirt and would get so muddy in the rainy season that you couldn't drive on it. Barry saw kids with plastic bags on feet instead of shoes and beggars in the streets. He heard the constant noise of traffic and street vendors, smelled diesel fuel everywhere.

As a child, Barack lived in Indonesia, the world's largest island country.

At 16 Haji Ramli Tengah Street they came to a small concrete house with a flat red-tiled roof and a fence in front. This would be their home. It had unreliable electricity, no air conditioning, and a primitive toilet. But it also had mango and pine trees in front, and a menagerie in back.

Lolo collected animals and kept chickens and lizards in the fenced backyard and even had a crocodile.

Barry had his own room, even if it was barely larger than a closet. It got really dark that night between the few streetlights, and now there was the scent of everyone's cooking: mostly fried rice and spicy beef.

Ann took him to walk on their street and meet their neighbors the next morning. They met their neighbor Ibu Ita, who was intrigued with this very white woman with her dark son. Barry immediately liked Ibu Ita's daughter, Dara. She was just his age. Soon he was hanging out at her house all the time. Once he hid under Dara's bed so he could stay and play longer.

Barry met and played with other kids, and ate everything everyone else ate. That meant eating snake, roasted grasshopper, and even dog.

Barack's (middle) kindergarten class included Japanese, Filipino, and Caucasian children and was led by Miss Sakai and her teacher's aid (top left).

Ann enrolled Barry in the Indonesian school. He learned to speak and read Indonesian in school but Ann woke him up early to teach him things he would need to know when he returned to America.

His friends were the children of government officials and the poorer children whose parents worked in fields and factories. His dark skin was an oddity in Jakarta. Kids were mostly curious about him, but he did get teased, and once some boys threw him in the swamp, and he had to swim out. But Barack was big and strong for his age. He shrugged it off.

Ann taught Barry about respect for others who are different, about Martin Luther King and Mahalia Jackson, a gospel singer who played an important role in the civil rights movement. Lolo taught him how farm animals are raised, and butchered, and how to fight and protect himself.

In two years Barry entered a different school, Besuki elementary. Their stucco house on Haji Ramli Street in Jakarta was in a crowded middle-class neighborhood.

Barry was getting known for his eagerness in school by the third grade. He always had his hand up. "Saya bu, saya!" he would shout. "Pick me Miss, pick me!" Or, "Ibu, boleh saya bantu hapus?" Meaning, "May I help you erase the blackboard?"

As a class assignment, he wrote an essay. Translated into English, it said:

While in Indonesia, Ann Dunham taught her son to be polite and a good listener.

"I am a third-grade student at SD Asisi. My mom is my idol. My teacher is Ibu Fer. I have a lot of friends. I live near the school. I usually walk to the school with my mom, then go home by myself. Someday I want to be president. I love to visit all the places in Indonesia. Done. The eeeeeeeend."

When he was nine, his sister Maya was born. By this time Barry was totally a part of the community. With his friends, he ran through the alleyways, ate crickets and hot green peppers, dodged three-foot-long lizards in the swamps, flew kites, and watched puppet shows. He was a part of it all, but he was also always observing and thinking about what he was seeing.

Then one summer, Ann decided it was time for Barry to continue his education in the United States. And Barry was sent back to Hawaii to live with his grandparents.

In 1966, Barack loved pretending to be a Major League baseball player.

Chapter 3
Stan and Toot

When Barry finished fourth grade, his mother put him on a plane. He was going back to Hawaii to stay with Grandpa Stan and Grandma Toot for the summer. He'd done that the summer before, but this time was different. In the fall he was to enroll in school in Hawaii. The Indonesia adventure was over for him. He was going to live in Hawaii now.

Stan and Toot lived in Punahou Circle Apartments, a high-rise apartment building a few blocks from the university. Toot was a vice president at a bank now, and was in her office all day. Stan had started selling life insurance. That meant he got to move around a lot, and often he took Barry with him. Sometimes this meant taking him along to smoky bars and meeting Stan's friends. One time Stan took Barry to meet a friend of his, a jazz fan named Frank Davis. Frank was black and Stan thought Barry should know someone with skin like his own.

School was starting in the fall, and Stan and Toot and Ann all wanted to get Barry into Punahou, an expensive private school four blocks from their apartment. Stan talked to his boss and Grandma Toot got some help from her boss at the bank. Obama had an interview with the school and took part in the scholarship program. His mother never gave up either. Finally, Barry got accepted.

Punahou was the most prestigious school in Hawaii and it had everything: a glass-blowing shed, a big swimming pool, tennis courts, and basketball courts. That sounds ritzy, but this was Hawaii, everybody dressed like they just got back from the beach.

Punahou took pride in its diversity, and there were kids in his class with names like Nunu, Kaui, Sigfried, Malia, Manu, Saichi, Wada, and Kalele. But when his teacher told the class that Barry's father was from Kenya, one kid asked if his father was a cannibal. Barry said his father was an African prince.

Barry didn't really know much about his father, and he was uncomfortable talking about him with the other kids. He was also curious about him. His mother had painted a romantic picture based on Harry Belafonte, a famous singer from Jamaica, and other famous black men. But Barry wondered what his father was really like.

He was soon to find out. In October of that year, 1971, his mother and sister arrived from Indonesia and rented an apartment near Stan and Toot. Then, a month later, his father, Barack Obama Sr., came from Kenya for a visit. Barry's first impression was that he was thin, and didn't look very healthy.

He didn't like how his father tried to boss him around. Stan stood up for Barry and said nobody could order anyone around in his house. Ann tried to make peace. There was a disturbing scene where Barry entered a room and saw his father angry and his mother in tears. It wasn't a totally happy visit.

But there were good times, too. Ann had described his father as smart and impressive and Barry soon decided that he lived up to his reputation. His father taught him to dance and joked with him and took him to a Dave Brubeck concert, which he really enjoyed. He decided he liked jazz. For Christmas, his father gave him a basketball. He really liked that, too.

And then Barry's teacher invited his father to speak to their class. Barry was embarrassed. He had told his classmates stories about his father, stories that weren't true. He knew so little about his father. Now they would find out that he had lied.

But his father impressed everyone, so that turned out mostly all right. Then it was time for his father to return to Kenya. It would turn out that Barry would never see him again. That spring his mother made plans to return to Indonesia for the summer. She needed to do anthropology research there. She also loved the country and the people and her work there. She felt more at home there than in Hawaii.

It was another summer living with Stan and Toot. When Barry started the sixth grade that fall, Ann and Maya were back in Hawaii. Ann was now in graduate school studying anthropology at the university. For the next three years Barry lived with his mother and sister in Honolulu.

His little sister was old enough to have fun with now, and she enjoyed playing with her big brother Barry. They both loved the frequent picnics with Stan and Toot.

At school, Barry got interested in tennis. Until the insult. One day he was looking at the sheet that had been posted showing rankings for tennis, and traced his name with his finger. The tennis pro came over and told him not to touch the sheet because he would get it dirty. Barry and his friends understood that it was a racial insult. "What do you mean by that?" Barry asked. The pro tried to pass it off as a joke, but Barry and his friends knew better.

With that insult, Barry lost interest in tennis. But there was the basketball his father had given him, and he soon found he had a talent for the game. He would play with his friends before and after school, and during breaks. They would play at school, on public courts near his grandparents' home, and in the university gym. He was quick and getting tall, and he had the weight to block the other kids and drive in for the shot. Basketball was becoming an important part of who he was.

A photo shoot of Barack from high school featured him in a coat, which was out of place in Honolulu.

After three years, his mother passed her exams and moved back to Indonesia with Maya, to do the field research she needed to complete her degree. And to live. Barry moved back in with his grandparents.

Chapter 4
<u>Basketball</u>

Freshmen at Punahou were assigned to a homeroom and they kept that same homeroom for the next four years. Barry's homeroom teacher was Mr. Kusunoki, but Barry called him "Mr. Kuz."

Barry was getting sure of himself. He had a style. He would come into homeroom first thing in the morning walking like his favorite basketball player, Dr. J. He'd have a book or two in one hand and a basketball in the other. "Hello, Mr. Kuz," he'd say, "How you doing?" He was always polite and cheerful, and his friends saw him as cool and thoughtful.

Now that he was in high school he was really into basketball — and he was good. It was just neighborhood games at first. He and his friends would get together to play in a basketball court on campus. They called themselves the Hack League. Later he got on one of the school teams, although at first this was the second-level team.

Barry made close friendships in high school. He and a friend named Bobby liked to go hiking in the hills above the school. Of course there was the beach. He and his friends would go body surfing on Sandy Beach. This was risky. Sandy Beach was known as "breakneck beach" because there were more injuries there than on any other beach in Hawaii.

Barack's basketball hero was hall of famer Julius Erving (Dr. J.). As a teenager, Obama even tried to walk like him.

Barry and his friends made spending money working summers scooping ice cream at Baskin-Robbins or serving slices at Mama Mia Pizza Parlor. They spent some of it going to a new movie called *Star Wars*.

Barack loved to body surf and returned with his family for many vacations in Hawaii as an adult.

Barry was growing more confident in his abilities. That definitely included his ability to debate. Mostly he got into arguments with Grandpa Stan, and Barry usually won. None of the arguments were really important, he just enjoyed exercising his arguing ability. And winning. He liked to win.

If Barry was ever worried about anything, his friends didn't know it. He kept some things to himself. With his mom not around much, he stopped mentioning that she was white. He thought it just complicated things. Kids who didn't know him well and saw him with his grandparents assumed he was adopted. He didn't correct them. He was just Barry; he didn't need to be the Black kid with the White mom.

He was a good student but didn't stand out. History and literature interested him, and a law course. Not so much the science classes. He was a good writer, though. It came easily to him. He would watch and observe and absorb and reflect on things like a writer. He could write a good paper on any subject the night before it was due.

His exposure to jazz music stuck with him. Maybe it was a connection with his father, or with being Black. In his senior year he and friend Greg Orme would go to Toot and Stan's after school and raid the fridge and read and listen to jazz in Barry's room.

That year he finally got onto the AA varsity basketball team. This was a big deal. That team was the best in the State. From December to March, basketball dominated his life: six days a week, two hours a day of practice.

He was good, but others on the team were good too, maybe better. Barry wasn't getting a lot of game time, and made an appointment

"Barry O'Bomber" was his nickname on his varsity basketball team because he would take difficult shots.

with Coach McLachlin to discuss it. Out on the playground, playing one-on-one, he knew he could beat a lot of these guys who were getting more game time. But Coach McLachlin taught a more disciplined game. Barry didn't win that argument, but it didn't bother him too much.

Finally, it was the State championship game. Thousands of people were there for the big game, and the Punahou team won it 60 – 28. Barry contributed just two of the points. He didn't mind not being in the game a lot. Through the the season he had learned some things about being a team player.

And he tried to learn something about what it meant to be Black. It was important to him to understand. He thought of his playing style as jazz-influenced. Was that part of what it meant to be Black?

But being in an exclusive school in a state and city that prided itself on diversity didn't make it easier. He was in one of the places in America where having dark skin was not a handicap. He was in a bubble, though he didn't really understand that yet.

Chapter 5
College

While attending Occidental College in Los Angeles,
Obama gave his first political speech.

The fall of 1979, Barry enrolled in college at
Occidental College in Los Angeles, California.
Even though he was away from home and on
the mainland and in college, he didn't find the
experience all that different. The Occidental
campus felt like Punahou. It was small, friendly,

and separate from the noise and bustle of LA. The weather in southern California was not too different from Hawaii, and if the ocean was a little farther away, it was still close enough that he and his new friends could drive down to Newport Beach to go body surfing now and then. He even had the chance to play basketball pretty much every day. The coach knew he had been a good player in high school and encouraged him, along with a dozen or so other freshmen. They used the gym for pick-up games when it was available.

The new friends he was making were a lot like his old friends. Here, too, he was drawn to foreign students, people who were different. His dorm was very diverse and filled with people from varied backgrounds. Barry, who had lived in Indonesia, had a father from Africa, and was mostly raised by his Anglo grandparents, seemed to find something in common with all of them. He had two roommates: Paul, a blond California surfer dude; and Imad, a Pakistani who had gone to secondary school in England and spoke with a proper British accent.

The dorm room had three beds, three desks, closets, and a sink. The bathroom was down the hall. Each of the students had his own typewriter, and everybody in the dorm had records and most had a record player.

Barry listened to Jimi Hendrix and Billie Holliday and the Rolling Stones. He was soon famous throughout the dorm for his impression of Mick Jagger, strutting and posing. He was enjoying playing it cool. An older student, a young woman who had developed a reputation for her photography, thought he was cool too. She had him pose for her in a series of photos, wearing funny hats and playing different roles.

This was all fun, but he soon started seeking out a different group of students. He found a coffee shop on campus called the Cooler, where artists and writers hung out, and it became his new hangout as well. He was discussing philosophy and politics and writing.

Sometimes, drawing on his experience arguing with Stan and debating in high school, he got into deep arguments about the CIA and writers like James Joyce and Kafka. In a political science class he impressed the upperclassmen with his debating skills. He argued like a lawyer, one of them thought.

Politics and writing were increasingly the focus of his attention. Once, when he had a paper due the next day in political science, a classmate asked if he had written it yet. "I've written it," he said, "I just haven't written it down." That night he stayed up late and wrote the paper. He got an A+. One classmate said he had a "magic pen."

Occidental College taught its students to approach problems with a three-word formula: listen, analyze, decide. Barry Obama already operated that way.

That year, his mother wrote to him that she and Lolo were getting divorced. Barry wasn't surprised.

In his second year he rented an apartment with his friend Hasan Chandoo from the African nation of Ghana. Soon, Barry and Hasan's apartment was the place for all the Pakistani

One of Barack's closest college friends,
Hasan Chandoo, was from Pakistan.

students on campus to hang out. They were
Barry's best friends. He saw in them a kind of
internationalism, like they were citizens of the
world. He identified with them.

Another friend, Eric Moore, gave Barry a
curious kind of connection with his father. Eric,
who was African-American, had actually been
to Kenya, and to the same part of Kenya where
Barry's father was from. The same place where
Barry had a lot of relatives he had never met and
knew nothing about. Eric had spent two months

in Kenya as a volunteer for Operation Crossroads Africa. Barry was fascinated to learn about Kenya from Eric. But Eric also had American experience that Barry didn't. "He was more Hawaiian and Asian and international," Eric said later, "than ... African American, because he hadn't had an urban African American experience at all."

Eric and Barry listened to a lot of music together, especially Bob Marley. One day Eric questioned Barry about his name. "Barry Obama," he said, "what kind of name is that for a brother?" Barry admitted that his name was really Barack, but it was easier to go by Barry. He didn't have to explain his name to people that way. Only now he was having to explain it to Eric. And Eric said, "If your name is Barack Obama, I'm going to call you Barack Obama," and he did. And Barry started thinking of himself as Barack.

He was spending more time at the Cooler now, and getting into more political discussions. And he was reading a lot of books by and about important Black figures in history. He was comfortable in an international, multicultural setting, and he was accepted there. He wasn't quite as accepted in places like UJIMA, a Black student group on campus named after a principle of Kwanzaa. Some of the members looked on Barack and Eric Moore as not Black enough. Barack was still searching for his Black identity.

That winter he gave his first public political appearance. There was a rally on campus against the apartheid policies in South Africa, and Barack gave a speech.

"There's a struggle going on," he said, "It's happening an ocean away. But it's a struggle that touches each and every one of us, whether we know it or not. A struggle that demands we choose sides."

And he was writing. The first issue of a new student literary magazine featured two poems signed by Barack Obama.

Those two things: politics and writing. He knew he was good at writing, and he thought he might be good at politics, but he had a lot of questions about it. That spring, he began to feel that he had a destiny, that something was expected of him. It was time to get serious. And that meant leaving the comfort and easiness of Occidental College.

These two years at Occidental had been great, he was finding things too easy, academically and socially. At the beginning of his Junior year, he transferred to Columbia University in New York City. This was a bigger change than going from Punahou High School to Occidental College.

Columbia in 1981 is where Barack got the experiences that Eric Moore thought he was missing. On his first night in New York, he found that he didn't have the key to the apartment he'd rented, and he spent the night sleeping in an alley. When he did get into the apartment, it was cold, small, and overrun with cockroaches. His walk to campus passed through tough neighborhoods.

It was just what he wanted, what he thought he needed. He needed to toughen up, to get serious. Now he was taking responsibility, pinching pennies, figuring out how to eat cheaply.

Although Columbia University in New York City is respected and famous, Obama was its first student to be elected President of the United States.

There was still time for some basketball and music. Now and then there were pick-up games. And when he could, he dropped in at the West End jazz club. He liked the music and the scene, but it was also about finding his black identity.

Meanwhile, he got really serious about his studies. He was a familiar figure walking across campus in his bomber jacket, always carrying books. There was always a book now, he would be studying while eating. He started keeping a journal, recording his thoughts, poems, short stories.

The two years at Columbia went quickly, but he grew up a lot in those years. One day he got a phone call from a woman in Kenya. She was his sister, and told him their father had died. The father that he really didn't know very well.

On graduation, Barack knew what he needed to do. He had to work with the poor, in Black communities, improving people's lives, helping them gain power. Chicago, he decided, was the city for a young Black man to make a difference in the world. He sent out letters to social service agencies about work, especially community organizing. He skipped graduation ceremonies, thinking them too frivolous. It was time to get serious about life.

Chapter 6
<u>In Chicago</u>

When Obama graduated from college in 1983, he went looking for work. His dream of changing the world would have to wait.

He found work at some boring jobs, but he kept looking. He wanted to work in community organizing, getting people in a community together to work toward a common goal.

A community organizer might be working with a political party to get a candidate elected

Chicago is Barack's adopted city. It's famous for many firsts, including the nation's first skyscraper in 1885.

one day and getting a stoplight installed at a dangerous intersection in the neighborhood the next day. Obama wanted to do all of that.

To find a place in community organizing, Obama wrote to community organizations all over the country offering his services. He had no luck at first. Then one organization, the Developing Communities Project, a church-based organization on Chicago's South Side, offered him an interview.

Obama interviewed with Gerald Kellman. Kellman was impressed with Obama's questions. "He wanted to know things like 'How are you going to train me?' and 'What am I going to learn?' "

Obama would later call his time working as an organizer "the best education I ever had."

That education took several different forms. For one thing, Obama started to learn about the way politics really works. In Chicago, he found, it wasn't always the people elected to office who had the power to get things done. Sometimes it was the people behind the scenes, who were out there working in the community.

Chicago was teaching Obama something about himself. Until now, he had always been a student. He had lived in different places and didn't really feel like any of them were home.

In Chicago, he found the real world outside of school, with all kinds of different people with different goals. And he found himself in a world that knew nothing about his complicated background. For the first time, he was simply a Black man in a big American city.

Gerald Kellman hired 24-year-old Barack Obama for his first job as a Chicago community organizer.

"Where I work, in the South Side," Obama said, "You go ten miles in any direction and not see a single white face. This was the result of segregation, but it also gave Obama something interesting, a black community that included people in many different economic conditions.

Not everyone was on welfare. Not everyone had dropped out of school. Not everyone was on drugs. Unlike what the newspaper headlines would suggest, there were neighborhoods of homeowners with stable jobs in the South Side. There were neighborhoods where neighbors helped each other out. Obama found a culture that offered something meaningful to its people, even to an outsider like a community organizer who hadn't yet settled down.

But Chicago was changing. Working-class neighborhoods were being hurt by the closing of the steel mills that provided good jobs. The changes were hurting working-class people regardless of their race.

For a community organizer, this was a chance to find the kind of common ground between the black and white communities. Their common problems might actually make them work together toward common goals.

But bridging the racial divide in America is tough. The situation on the South Side gave Obama hope that he might build at least a small, rickety bridge. In the end, he didn't accomplish any miracles in his three years in town. Chicago made more of a difference to Obama than Obama did to Chicago.

But he did have some successes as a community organizer. During his time in Chicago, he helped set up both a pre-college tutoring program and a jobs training program. He also worked as an advocate for tenants' rights, supporting the tenants of one of Chicago's public housing projects.

That project, known as Altgeld Gardens, was a village of 1500 apartments built for African-American veterans returning home from World War II.

By the time Obama was working with the tenants, Altgelt Gardens was a poor place to raise a family. It was surrounded by industrial sites and waste dumps. Pollution was a big problem. On top of that, the walls and ceilings of the buildings were lined with asbestos, a major health hazard.

Obama to set up a meeting that attracted 700 residents, all assembled in a stifling gym and awaiting the opportunity to confront the Chicago Housing Authority's director, who had promised to attend.

The director arrived more than an hour late. The crowd, already angry, became more angry. They yelled at the director. He left. To Obama, it felt like a complete disaster.

Maybe it was not as bad as he thought, though. The city did take eventually get rid of the asbestos. Obama's work played a part in setting the wheels in motion. His frustrations, though, were one reason that he'd leave Chicago behind in 1988, returning to a place very different from the world he was leaving behind.

Chapter 7
In Kenya

Obama's time in Chicago as a young man had a significant influence on his identity, an influence that made itself felt in two different ways.

First, it had a very specific influence on his career plans. It was his first exposure to life as a community organizer in the real world. He came face to face with the frustrations of working with all kinds of people with all kinds of problems.

It was hard to keep people involved in working toward change, simply because of the energy it took from people.

One of the last things he heard from an Altgeld tenant was that "ain't nothing gonna change" and that the best thing to do was to save up enough money to move out of the project to a better place.

Chicago may well have answered any questions he had about life on the front lines of community organizing. Perhaps this was not the career he'd hoped it would be.

Second, it was his first real exposure to something he hadn't known. A big and black community that saw him as one of its own.

In many ways, this was a new experience. Before Chicago, Obama was seen as multi-ethnic, multi-cultural kid who had lived in several different parts of the world and who didn't really have a fixed identity. In the United States alone, he'd lived in Hawaii, California and New York City. Where would he call home? In Chicago, he began answering that question. Chicago took him as an African-American and seemed to have no doubt about it.

There was, of course, a catch. Obama was actually a bit different than most of the African-Americans he met. Most of them, it's safe to say, were the descendants of slaves. Many of them found themselves in Chicago because of the Great Migration, the movement of millions of blacks from the South to the North that happened between 1916 and 1970, with Chicago as one of its most popular landing places.

Obama's story was different, his connection to Africa more immediate. Barack Obama Senior, had come to America of his own free will in 1959. He had been mostly absent from his son's life, leaving the family when Obama the younger was still a toddler.

Barack Obama Senior, had died in a car crash in Africa back in 1982, when Obama was in college. Nevertheless, he was an important piece of Obama's identity, even as a missing piece. Obama's African roots were, in a sense, more immediate than those of most African-Americans in Chicago and elsewhere in the United States.

In 1987, Obama took a trip to Kenya that he hoped might help to fill in some of that missing piece of his family and his heritage. As he tells the story in *Dreams From My Father*, that trip had two dramatic effects on his sense of himself.

The first one happened before he had even left the airport, when the name "Obama" was immediately recognized by the woman who met him there. For the first time, he felt "the comfort...that a name might provide, how it could carry an entire history." The name that had been strange and foreign in America, one that people often got wrong, was homey and familiar to an ordinary Kenyan.

That was one part of Obama's sense of belonging. The other was his experience of Africa as a black person among other black people. Here, everyone, or almost everyone, looked like him. He was no longer an outsider in the larger culture.

In Kenya, Swahili and English are the two official languages, but dozens of other languages are spoken.

He could leave behind the black-white divide. A sense of being watched and the feeling of being different that are so much a part of African-American life. In this way, too, a part of Obama had found something like a home away from home.

Obama spent several weeks in Kenya. He met and visited with all sorts of people who were part of his extended African family, spending time at their homes, drinking tea and talking. Much of the talk centered on his father and grandfather. One of his last stops in Kenya was a visit to their graves, which sit side by side in a spot close to the village that was the Obama clan's home. It is the village of Kogelo.

For most of a day, Obama sat with his step-grandmother. He listened as she told him the story of the family through the generations, ending with the stories of Obama's own grandfather and father.

These two men had lived through the rise and fall of the British colonization of Kenya. They were men whose lives had been difficult and troubled, and men who had left little of material value behind for Barack himself.

While in Kenya, Barack met many family members like his grandmother Sarah, stepsister Auma, and stepmother Kezia.

They had left a legacy, though, and it was a legacy that made Obama weep as he sat between the simple, unadorned graves. He wept because the trip had taught him something about who he was and what he cared about. It had also revealed to him the reality of his father, a man who he had idealized for many years. Now he heard the full story of his father from the people who knew it. The man was often a terrible husband and father, one who gave in to drunken rages and who was bitter beyond words about his failures and his life.

This was a side of his father that Obama hadn't known, but, while disappointing, it affected him in a positive way. For the first time, he felt connected to the same pain his father had felt. He felt connected to the struggles of that father and millions like him. Finally, to the personal struggles Obama himself had lived with.

For Obama, the time in Kenya meant that who he was and what he cared about were no longer thoughts. They were deeply felt. "I saw that my life in America – the black life, the white life, the sense of abandonment I'd felt as a boy, the frustration and hope I'd witnessed in Chicago – all of it was connected to this small plot of earth an ocean away."

No matter how much all this meant to him, however, Obama was not about to settle in Kenya and live his life in Africa. By this time, he already had plans to cross that ocean again. He was ready to return to America and begin a new chapter in the place that was still, for better or worse, his true home.

Chapter 8
At Harvard

The gulf between the Kenyan village of Kogelo and the Massachusetts city of Cambridge, home of the renowned Harvard Law School, is vast. The distance between them is measured in more than miles.

Barack attended Harvard Law School. Graduates of this great school include many Supreme Court Judges.

When he came home from his trip to Kenya, Obama faced a new challenge. He was about to spend three years in an academic environment that was famously tough. His classmates were all the best and brightest and competition was fierce. As it happened, he adapted to life as a law student without missing a beat.

The first year of law school is devoted to a few standard courses meant to educate students in basic principles. It can be hard for a first year student to stand out for anything other than getting excellent grades. Obama certainly got the grades. He graduated with high honors, but he was distinctive in a different way as well. That difference is remembered by one of his most famous professors, Laurence Tribe.

Tribe is a "rock star" of constitutional law, well known around the school for his reluctance to take on first year students as assistants. Obama wanted to work with him. Toward the end of his first year, Obama asked to meet with Tribe.

That meeting landed Obama a job as Tribe's primary research assistant, and Obama worked on complex legal articles, including one that somehow connected constitutional law and quantum physics. Tribe was impressed.

At Harvard, Barack became a research assistant
for Professor Lawrence Tribe. Tribe later became an adviser
to Barack's 2008 presidential campaign.

Many years later, Tribe came across his old
calendar from 1989. There, on March 31, was
the name "Obama," followed by an exclamation
point and a phone number. As Tribe recalls, that
exclamation point was meant as a reminder of
how impressed he had been by Obama from the
very start.

One thing that set Obama apart was his age. He had come to law school at 27, and he had arrived there not only after his eye-opening trip to Kenya, but after his stint in Chicago as a community organizer. Unlike most of his classmates, who tended to be fresh out of college, Obama had lived in the "real world" for years. That experience showed.

Obama's time outside of school did more than make him a few years older than his classmates. His experience dealing with Chicago politics led to a lasting interest in how systems worked in the real world. He understood how those systems could do so much to help people if you knew how to use them. Law school could teach Barack that.

His real-world experience made him appreciate the art of compromise. In Chicago, Obama's attempts to make things better for the community were often frustrated. Compromise might not give you everything you wanted, but you could get a little here if you were willing to give a little there. That approach, though, meant that you had to see things through the opposition's eyes. It takes some maturity and experience to make that leap.

In law school, that experience must have encouraged Obama to adopt a mindset that was less interested in confrontation and more interested in bringing people together through compromise. That attitude would be part of his nature, for better or worse, for decades to come.

According to his classmates, it was that attitude that helped him to reach the first of his historic milestones, election as the first black president of the *Harvard Law Review*.

In almost every law school in America, the law review is a scholarly publication staffed by students in their second and third years. At Harvard, membership is offered to the students who have excelled in their first year. Only a few dozen make it out of a class of more than 500.

If it's an honor to make law review; it's an even greater honor to be elected the organization's president. Votes are cast by second-year and third-year students on the review. Anyone in his or her second year can run. The voters know the candidates well. They've all spent a great deal of time at the review's offices during that second year, doing the kind of grunt work that it takes to publish any academic publication. The work is far from glamorous, but it provides a chance for people get to know each other deeply.

Politics plays an important part in voters' thinking. Lines are drawn between liberal and conservative factions.

You might think that liberal-minded Obama would share that view and that it was the liberal side that would swing the election in his favor. In fact, though, something different happened. When the last remaining conservative candidate had left the race, the entire conservative faction swung over to support Obama's candidacy.

They didn't move in that direction because they thought Obama was one of them. Instead, they saw him as someone who would still respect their views even if he disagreed. It was Obama's respect for the opposition and his willingness to work with people with whom he didn't see eye to eye that won the day.

At the Review's annual banquet at the Harvard Club, Obama spoke to the banquet about his election and how it had been a breakthrough for everyone. It was not just for him and not just for African-Americans. The room that night was itself a reflection of the world around it. A group of diners that was largely white and a contingent of waiters that was largely black. Both groups listened intently, and both applauded when Obama had finished. In the midst of the applause, one of those black waiters, an older man, rushed up to shake Obama's hand.

That was almost certainly another first in the law review's history.

The simple fact that he was elected led to a book deal. That's Obama, something that's almost completely unheard of for someone who had yet to graduate from law school. It came about because a literary agent in New York City read an article about the law review election.

She suggested that Obama consider writing a book, something about history, law and race in America, perhaps. She managed to interest a major publisher in the project.

It would be a few years before the book appeared. When it did, it wasn't the kind of historical study you might expect from an alumnus of the *Harvard Law Review*. Instead, it was Obama's personal story, *Dreams From My Father*, an autobiography that was a much more

Barack made headlines for the first time while at Harvard when he became the first African American elected president of the law school's prestigious law review.

personal project than anything that agent had in mind. But Obama received a substantial amount of money when the deal was made, something of a dream come true for a law student who didn't have family money.

It might seem like Obama's years in law school were all about ambition, academics and career. Obama has talked about the long hours spent in dimly lit libraries, but there was something else happening at the same time. It involved a woman who had graduated from Harvard Law in 1988, just before Obama arrived on campus.

That woman was Michelle Robinson. She'd grown up in Chicago with her brother Craig in a family well-known within the community. The Robinson family had come to Chicago as part of the Great Migration. They lived on the South Side, and they were rooted in Chicago's black community.

A background more different than Obama's would be hard to imagine, but Michelle and Barack would find common ground. When they first met, she was working at a major Chicago law firm. He had gone there for a summer job, and she was his summer adviser at the firm.

Michelle Robinson grew up with her parents and brother Craig on Chicago's south side.

They had lunch, and Michelle wasn't expecting much, just another one of those "smooth brothers who could talk straight and impress people," as she said years later.

Instead, they clicked. They spent a day together, including a stop at the Art Institute. Lunch at the museum and a viewing of Spike Lee's movie, *Do the Right Thing*. They finished up with ice cream on the way home. They shared a first kiss. That turned out to be the start of something big, and they would share much more in the years to come.

"Just try new things. Don't be afraid.
Step out of your comfort zone," Michelle Obama has said.

Chapter 9
Teacher and Activist

In 1991, Barack Obama graduated from Harvard Law School near the top of his class, earning the distinction magna cum laude, meaning "with great honor." Because of this and his being president of the law review, he had many job offers to choose from. He could join a big law firm with rich clients and make a lot of money. He could work for a Supreme Court Justice and start on a path to being a judge.

To Barack, these opportunities all came down to a basic choice, was he more interested in money and fame or in working to help people? He knew what he was going to do. He was going to return to Chicago and continue the kind of work he had already started there, working to help people in the African-American community. Chicago was a place where he thought he could make a real difference.

The fact that Michelle Robinson was in Chicago was one more reason he wanted to go there.

Barack and Michelle met in Chicago while he did an internship following his first year of law school.

When it came to choosing a specific job, though, he had a harder time deciding. He thought he'd like to teach. That was a way to give back, to make a difference. He wanted to use his law degree to help people in trouble, which maybe meant working for a law firm. And he wanted to make a difference in Chicago politics. In the end, he took on three jobs.

He accepted a teaching position at the University of Chicago Law School, a part-time job he would keep for twelve years, teaching a variety of topics including Constitutional Law.

He also took a job at a Chicago law firm that specialized in civil rights cases. The firm, then known as Davis, Miner, Barnhill & Galland, defended people's voting rights, represented tenants against landlords and employees against business owners. They generally looked out for the little guy.

Barack and Project Vote worked hard to help people register to vote, adding more than 150,000 new African American voters in 1992.

A bit later, he signed up to work for Project Vote, helping get people registered to vote. Oh, and he was also working on that book he had agreed to write, and thinking about going into politics.

It was a good thing neither the University nor the law firm expected him to be there full-time.

He and Michelle were dating, and she wasn't so sure about some of his choices. Michelle was working in community organizations helping people, and working long hours herself. But she argued that politics wasn't a good way to try to make a difference. She was skeptical of politicians. She was proud of Barack and pushed him to be sure of his choices.

1992 was a big election year, and the Project Vote people wanted him to work long hours. They made it clear that they needed every hour he could give them to get out there encouraging people to register. He kept up with his classes at the law school, but he cut back on work at the law firm, and he put his book aside completely until after the election.

Project Vote gave him some money to get started, and he set up an office and recruited people to go out and register voters. He trained 700 of these people in how to do this. He talked to leaders in the African-American community.

Some of them were not impressed by this young man who hadn't grown up in Chicago and thought he could come into their city and advise them on how to get people voting.

But gradually, he overcame their resistance. He made friends with influential community leaders and political workers. He did a good job with Project Vote, and people started to pay attention to this young man with the unusual name. Michelle knew what all this meant. He was going to go into politics.

Just before the 1992 election, they got married. For the next four years, they were an idealistic young couple, using their Harvard Law School degrees to work in the community.

Barack and Michelle got married in 1992.

Barack had found in Michelle something he had been missing all his life, identification with a community. He loved her family. Her hard-working father had died the year Barack had moved to Chicago. Her mother Marian was Barack's idea of what a mother should be. Her brother Craig was a genuine basketball star, something Barack could really relate to. They represented stability and reliability that Barack had missed growing up.

Barack's own mother, who was so often absent from his life, died in 1995 from uterine cancer at 52 years old.

During these years at the law firm Barack worked on about thirty cases. Most of the work was writing motions and preparing depositions. Once in a while he argued a case in court. In one case he went up against Citibank, suing the big bank for discriminating against minorities in its lending practices.

In his law school classes, he had his students debate interracial marriage and adoption, voting challenges for minorities, discrimination in sentencing of people convicted of crimes. He had them read Martin Luther King's famous "Letter from Birmingham Jail," an important text in the American Civil Rights Movement. Other teachers, liberal and conservative, praised his knowledge and fairness. He always got high ratings from his students. If he wanted to make teaching his full-time career, he could have.

And he was now a published author. His book, *Dreams from My Father*, was published in 1995 and was selling moderately well.

Michelle may have hoped that he would be satisfied with teaching and law work and writing, and forget about politics. But in 1996 he ran and was elected to the Illinois State Senate. Two years later, he was re-elected, and later, re-elected to a third term. During these years, their two daughters, Malia and Sasha were born. And then he decided to run for the United States Senate. Michelle wasn't happy about that. It was bad enough that he was away from home so much in Springfield, the capital of Illinois. If he became a Senator, he would spend a lot of his time in Washington, D.C., more than 600 miles away. Barack made a promise. "If I lose this," he told her, "I'm out of politics."

Like Barack, Michelle had a degree from Harvard Law, and like Barack, she had a strong work ethic and a passion to do good work. Michelle was a career woman now, working long hours, and her work was important to her. Barack understood. He didn't want to be an absentee dad. He knew what that was like. But people kept asking him to do more.

Barack got national attention with his keynote speech at the Democratic National Convention in 2004.

In 2004, when U. S. Senator John Kerry was running for President, he needed to pick someone to make the big keynote speech at the party convention. This was the kind of speech that could make a young politician famous on the national stage. Barack Obama was still just a State Senator, but people told Kerry that this young man was a rising star. Kerry asked him to give the speech. Barack knew what an opportunity this was.

The day of the convention arrived, and he took the stage. The crowd was noisy, not paying a lot of attention at first. He started out by telling his story, about his mixed background, about the dreams and difficulties his parents and grandparents had. He went on to connect his own story with everyone's story, and explained that this willingness to accept differences was the American story:

"It is that fundamental belief — I am my brother's keeper, I am my sister's keeper — that makes this country work. It's what allows us to pursue our individual dreams, yet still come

together as one American family: E pluribus unum, out of many, one."

Barack became a US Senator
and won 70% of the vote in the election of 2004.

Later that year, he was elected to the United States Senate. Barack Obama was going to Washington, DC.

Chapter 10
From Senator to President

Obama's election to the Senate was a real chance to expand his influence on a national scale. Many people had heard his rousing speech at the 2004 convention, but the fame it brought him could have faded if he'd ended his political career with that speech.

As a U.S. Senator, Obama was on the national stage, filling one of only 100 seats in the Senate.

His three years in the Senate were active years. He was involved in initiatives relating to immigration, the control of weapons around the world, election reform, the environment and the state of America's military.

For Obama, the job wasn't only about writing laws and working with his fellow Senators to get those laws passed. It was also a way to get a first-hand look at parts of the world that were important to America's foreign policy but that he'd never seen. In 2005, he traveled to Russia,

Ukraine, and Azerbaijan. The next year, he returned to Africa, revisiting Kenya and touring Djibouti, Ethiopia, Chad and South Africa, and travelled to the Middle East, visiting Jordan, Israel and the Palestinian territories.

One seemingly small aspect of his Senate career stood out in Obama's mind. Each Senator is assigned a desk in the Senate chamber, and they are the same desks used by Senators who have come before.

There are 100 members of the United States Senate, which met for the first time in 1789.

Obama was delighted to find that his desk had been occupied by, among others, Robert

Kennedy, President John F. Kennedy's younger brother. The younger Kennedy had served in the Senate for just three years before running for President in 1968.

As he became better known throughout the country, that seemed to be a story that Obama might be interested in repeating in his own life. That was a step, though, that first needed plenty of thought. Obama had a wife and children to consider. Gearing up for a national political campaign, and rising to the highest office in the land, would be asking a lot of everyone involved. Long days and nights of work, and long days and nights apart, were all part of what it takes to hit the campaign trail.

Life as a Senator was not exactly family-friendly. Barack and Michelle had decided that moving the family to Washington was not the best choice for the family, especially for the children. She had stayed in Chicago while he lived in Washington. They saw each other on the weekends and at holidays.

Barack was never satisfied with that kind of long-distance parenting. He wanted to be with his daughters while they were growing up. He'd been separated from his parents for some of his childhood, and it wasn't what he wanted for his girls or himself.

Nevertheless, people all over the country were letting Obama hear that the time was right for him to make a run at the Presidency. His name was all over the media as a potential candidate. If he was tempted to wait, to spend more time in the Senate, that might actually hurt his chances. He was hot now.

In the face of growing pressure, he worried about the loss of privacy that would only get worse if he campaigned, and what effect that would have on Malia and Sasha, not just on him and Michelle.

Toward the end of 2006, the family took a trip to Hawaii together, specifically to discuss what all this meant to their lives. By the time they returned, the decision was made, Obama would run, and he would announce his candidacy officially on February 10, 2007.

Barack came to realize that there might be a silver lining to the Presidency despite its demands. If nothing else, the family could dream of spending four years of living under the same roof together. The fact that it was the roof of the White House, and that there was an election to win made this decision a little different than most. However, it was the same general line of thought that might be on the mind of any father who didn't want to miss his daughters' childhoods.

The White House is the only home of a country's
leader that can be toured for free.
However, tours have to be booked beforehand.

Before any of this could happen, Obama had to win his party's nomination. Becoming the Democratic Presidential candidate meant winning state caucuses and primaries. This meant Barack had to convince each state that he was the best option among all of the candidates in the same party.

Barack ran for President while the country was entering a serious financial crisis.

This was a tough task in itself, because Obama faced some tough opposition. The toughest coming from Hillary Clinton. Was the Democratic Party ready to give an African-American candidate a real chance?

Barack and Michelle fiercely guarded the privacy of their daughters. During the presidential campaign, the girl's grandmother, Marian, drove the girls to school, fed them dinner, and tucked them into bed.

In the national election, Obama ran against another Senator, Republican John McCain of Arizona, who was in many ways Obama's opposite. He had already served in the Senate for more than 20 years. While McCain was seen as the candidate who offered more of the same, Obama portrayed his candidacy as something different from business as usual. He embodied "change we can believe in," as his campaign slogan promised.

While Obama's race certainly set him apart from candidates who had preceded him, his campaign was different for other reasons as well. It was the first campaign to rely heavily on modern technology. Taking advantage of the huge amounts of data available about prospective voters and using social media to help spread Barack's message.

In the end, the campaign was successful beyond what even Obama might have imagined.

When the ballots were counted on election day, Obama came away with 53 percent of the popular vote, the biggest share since 1988.

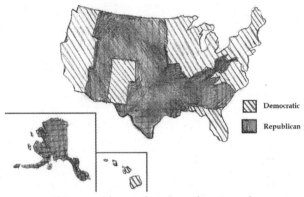

This map shows the areas that Barack won in 2008 to get elected to the presidency.

Americans had elected the first African-American President in the nation's history. "Change we can believe in" had come to pass.

Obama gave his victory speech in Chicago, where he had watched the election results come in. The crowd was estimated to be almost a quarter of a million people. He was well aware of what his victory meant.

He told the crowd, "If there is anyone out there who still doubts that America is a place where all things are possible, who still wonders if the dream of our founders is alive in our time, who still questions the power of our democracy, tonight is your answer."

Now, with the campaign behind him, he faced a new challenge. Could he bring people together to actually make the changes that they'd hoped for? Could he be the person he'd been trying to become, who was truly ready and able to lead the nation to a better future? There were real tests yet to come.

The Obamas—Barack, Sasha, Malia, and Michelle—were the first First Family of African American descent.

Chapter 11
Barack Obama as President

On November 4, 2008, Senator Barack Obama was declared the winner of the election against Senator John McCain and became the 44th President of the United States. He was re-elected for a second term four years later and from 2009–2017, he was President of the United States.

Before assuming office, Barack met with the 43rd President of the United States, his predecessor, President George W. Bush.

A modest man from humble roots, he had overcome racial prejudices to become the first African American president. His cheerful optimism with promises to change America for the better won over the hearts of Americans across the country. He overcame bigotry with intelligence, poise, and good will.

Before President George W. Bush passed the presidential torch to President Obama, the Obama family came to the White House. President Bush's daughters, Jenna and Barbara, gave the girls a tour, showing them a part of what being a First Child entailed. Their tour included showing them a solarium lamp that could be slid down like a fire pole and a hallway that doubles as an obstacle course.

Laura Bush took the time to show Michelle around. As the former First Lady, she understood part of the pressure and stress that having a husband as President can bring to a family. She showed Michelle the secret rooms and closets, including a secret door into the Oval Office.

The Obamas had Michelle's mom move into the White House
with the family to help raise their children.

The new First Family is allowed to redecorate
to fit a personal style. Before moving in, Barack
and Michelle informed designer Michael Smith
that the priorities were preparing bedrooms for
Malia, Sasha, and Michelle's mother, Marian
Robinson, to ensure they were comfortable
and happy.

Michelle Obama redecorated the old White
House dining room, updating it with art from

African American artists, the first to be displayed in the White House.

The new President insisted on one particular change, an expansion of the basketball court to full-court size. He wasn't going to give up an occasional pick-up game just because he was President of the United States.

One very aggressive play during a White House game ended up with Barack needing 12 stitches and sporting a split lip.

And the girls explored their new home. The White House, they were delighted to learn, has hidden rooms, a built-in movie theatre, and a personal chef available 24 hours a day. It was both a home and a playground for the Obama girls. In total the White House has 132 rooms, six different levels, 35 bathrooms, a total of 412 doors, and three elevators, making it a child's dream for adventures and exploring.

During the eight years Obama played host to hundreds of visiting world leaders and dignitaries. The President's days were filled with important meetings and difficult, important decisions.

The Obamas promised their girls they could have a dog if their father became President. They wound up with two.

As a gift from Senator Ted Kennedy, the Obamas family received a Portuguese water dog, named Bo. Bo was later joined by another dog of the same breed, Sunny. The breed is hypoallergenic so it was good for Malia who had allergies.

Though the White House is both office and home for the First Family, Barack and Michelle emphasized that their private quarters were a home and a place of fun and laughter for their children. The family was close and ate dinner as a family together, took regular family vacations, played sports and enjoyed time outdoors.

When President Obama began his first term he faced the challenge of helping the country out of the Great Recession, the worst economic crisis in the United States since the Great Depression of the 1930s. President Obama's economic program helped the country begin to turn around.

Obama promised to reform healthcare during his campaign and made good on his promise with the passing of the Affordable Care Act. The legislation made it possible for more than 20 million Americans to be able to purchase health insurance for their families.

When terrorists attacked the World Trade Center on September 11, 2001 (9/11), the country focused on the mastermind behind the plan: Osama bin Laden. President Obama approved the plan that resulted in the capture and death of bin Laden on May 2, 2011.

President Obama championed the DREAM Act, which would have made it possible for thousands of undocumented students to be able to finish their education and make a better life for themselves without fear of deportation.

The office of President has sometimes been marred with scandals and controversy, including the Teapot Dome scandal of President Warren Harding in 1922 and Richard Nixon's Watergate scandal in 1972.

When he took office, President Obama promised to uphold the highest office in the land with integrity. He fulfilled his promise, remaining relatively untouched by scandals during his eight years in the White House.

Barack, Sasha, Michelle, and Malia lived in the White House for eight years from 2013 to 2019.

Beginning on the first night of his presidency, President Obama asked his staff to bring him 10 letters each night from his constituents. The letters were from the youngest of children to the elderly. The letters helped him get a glimpse of the issues and concerns of the American citizens. He often visited the letter-writers while he travelled, connecting with them face-to-face.

It was a tough job, filled with challenges. And he didn't win all the battles.

During the eight years of his presidency, the United States became increasingly divided. Controversial topics, such as same-sex marriage and gun violence, pushed Americans farther apart from one another. During the first part of his presidency, Democrats controlled Congress, allowing President Obama to pass promised legislation. When Republicans took control of both the House and the Senate in 2015, President Obama struggled to get legislation passed.

President Obama won reelection in 2012 against Governor Mitt Romney of Massachusetts.

One day, an employee brought his five-year-old son to see the President. Little Jacob Philadelphia stood with his family while a picture was taken of them and the President. Jack, an African American, stared at President Obama and quietly asked if his hair felt like his own. The poignant picture of President Obama bending over to let Jack touch his air hung in the White House for years, a reminder of a country built on equality and opportunity for all.

President Obama enjoyed having children
visit him in the White House.

Again and again, President Obama found himself speaking after an episode of gun violence, often at a schools. He was frustrated and saddened that he was unable to get anything done to reduce these terrible events.

A President who continually pushed for change and hope in America, he ended his presidency with a warning to America in his farewell speech. He urged Americans to come together, to end divisions over race and to continue to fight for the democracy of the country. On January 20, 2017, President Obama officially turned over the baton of leading the country to the new President. In his farewell speech, he said:

> *"If I had told you eight years ago that America would reverse a great recession, reboot our auto industry, and unleash the longest stretch of job creation in our history. If I had told you that we would open up a new chapter with the Cuban people, shut down Iran's nuclear weapons program without firing a shot, and take out the mastermind of 9/11. If I had told you that we would win marriage equality, and secure the*

right to health insurance for another 20 million of our fellow citizens—you might have said our sights were set a little too high.

"But that's what we did. That's what you did. You were the change. You answered people's hopes, and because of you, by almost every measure, America is a better, stronger place than it was when we started."

President Obama met with President-elect
Donald Trump before leaving office.

Chapter 12
Legacy

The life of President Obama reads like a Hollywood script. Born in Hawaii, his journey would not only transport him to the heart of Chicago activism, but ultimately to the White House. As the first African American president, Obama jump-started change across racial, social, and political landscapes.

Throughout his eight years as Commander in Chief, Obama led the United States through harsh economic times and social progress. But, as the administration changed in 2017, the man who had graced the daily lives of Americans faded temporarily into the background.

The first thing the Obamas did was take a vacation. In the Virgin Islands, far away from the work and stress of Washington. The Obamas took some much needed time to enjoy a quieter life, which included kiteboarding, of course.

Imagine what life had been like for Sasha and Malia Obama, who were 7 and 10 years old when they moved into the most recognizable home in America. For the next eight years, the world watched as these young girls grew in to impressive young women.

Vacationing post-Presidency.

The older daughter, Malia, took a gap year before attending Harvard University and took an internship with a Hollywood production company, reading and evaluating scripts.

Meanwhile, Sasha graduated high school in 2019 and will attend the University. Although she's shown interest in many activities, the world has yet to see what the future holds for the youngest First Daughter.

First Lady, Michelle Obama had dedicated her years in the White House to advocacy. That wasn't so different from the work she had done before moving to Washington, and now that she is a private citizen again, she continues working for the causes she believes in. Her passion for helping the American people is as strong as ever. Michelle published a book in 2018 titled *Becoming*.

Like Michelle, Barack Obama had, before becoming President, been focused on community. When he left office, it didn't change his dedication. He immersed himself in the establishment of the Obama Foundation. Based in Chicago, this foundation is already making change in a city torn by decades of unchecked political and social upheaval.

The cornerstone of his post-presidency life is built around the creation of the Obama Presidential Center. Located in the South Side of Chicago, this center will boast a library, museum, education annex, and of course basketball courts, and acts as the headquarters for the Obama Foundation. Along with its newfound uses, the Obama Presidential Center will also serve as the main office for My Brother's Keeper Alliance, which continues a program Obama founded while President in 2014 to close opportunity gaps for boys and young men of color.

Obama explained:

"There's nothing, not a single thing, that's more important to the future of America than whether or not you and young people all across this country can achieve their dreams."

But you don't have to go to Chicago to keep up with the Obamas. Barack and Michelle are creating a series of podcasts you can listen to on Spotify and a series of movies you can watch on Netflix. Michelle says the podcasts will "amplify voices that are too often ignored or silenced altogether." And Barack says the movies "will educate, connect, and inspire us all," by "touching on issues of race and class, democracy, and civil rights." And some of the podcasts will feature the voices of both Obamas. Their first Netflix series was *American Factory*, a documentary series about a factory in Ohio.

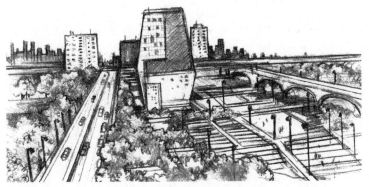

The Barack Obama Presidential Center will be located on the south side of Chicago.

"We've always believed in the value of entertaining, thought-provoking conversation," Barack says. "It helps us build connections with each other and open ourselves up to new ideas." And, Michelle adds, "help people connect emotionally and open up their minds—and their hearts."

Select Quotes from Barack Obama

"I don't oppose all wars. What I am opposed to is a dumb war. What I am opposed to is a rash war. A war based not on reason but on passion, not on principle but on politics."
—Thoughts on war, 2002

"Hope in the face of difficulty, hope in the face of uncertainty, the audacity of hope: in the end, that is God's greatest gift to us, the bedrock of this nation, a belief in things not seen, a belief that there are better days ahead."
—Democratic National Convention, 2004

"Change will not come if we wait for some other person or some other time. We are the ones we've been waiting for. We are the change that we seek."
—Speech to supporters, 2008

"We have a choice. We can shape our future or let events shape it for us. And if we want to succeed, we can't fall back on the stale debates and old divides that won't move us forward. Don't shortchange the future because of fear in the present."
—Speaking with Prime Minister Gordon Brown, 2009

"I believe in Nelson Mandela's vision. I believe in a vision shared by Gandhi and King and Abraham Lincoln. I believe in a vision of equality and justice and freedom and multiracial democracy, built on the premise that all people are created equal, and they're endowed by our creator with certain inalienable rights."
—Nelson Mandela Annual Lecture, 2018

Glossary

Alderman a member of a city legislative body.

Anglo a person of English descent.

Anthropology the science of human beings and especially their physical characteristics, their origin, their environment and social relations, and their culture.

Apartheid a policy of racial segregation formerly practiced in the Republic of South Africa (1948–1994).

Asbestos a grayish mineral that is used to make materials that are fireproof, and can cause serious lung disease if inhaled as a dust.

Bigotry the beliefs of those who regards the members of a group (especially racial groups) with hatred and intolerance.

Buddhism the religion originated by Buddha holding that suffering is caused by desire and that the way to end suffering is through enlightenment.

Campaign trail connected series of planned events taken on by a politician who wishes to be elected.

Cannibal an animal that eats the flesh of other animals in the same species.

Chad a country in North Central Africa, south of Libya. It was formerly a French territory that became independent in 1960.

Civil Rights the rights guaranteed to an individual like the right to vote, equal treatment, and freedom from slavery.

Colony a group of people who create a settlement in a distant land but remain under the governmental control of their native country.

Constituents any of the voters who elect a person to represent them.

Deposition the testimony of a witness made under oath, but not in open court, and written down to be used when the case comes to trial.

Discrimination the unjust treatment of people on the grounds of race, age, sex, or other features.

Djibouti a country in eastern Africa. Djibouti was a French colony that gained independence in 1977.

Factions a party group within a government.

Hinduism the principal religious tradition of India, characterized by the worship of many gods, a belief in reincarnation, and the concept of karma, or the cumulative effect of all of one's actions.

Immigrate coming into a foreign country to live permanently.

Independent nation countries that run themselves instead of relying on outside countries to legislate the country.

International trade the exchange of goods and services between countries.

Internationalism the principle or policy of international cooperation for the common good.

Legislation the act of making laws.

Menagerie a collection of wild or unusual animals.

Islam the monotheistic religion believing in Allah, and whose chief prophet and founder is Muhammad.

Plessy v. Ferguson the United States Supreme Court decision in 1896 that upheld laws of racial segregation. The phrase "separate but equal" was coined during this time.

Prestigious having a high reputation.

Revelation a surprising fact or event that makes you look at things in a new way.

Segregation the policy or practice of compelling racial groups to live apart from each other, go to separate schools, use separate facilities, etc.

South Africa the country in southernmost Africa.

Stopgap a temporary substitute.

Stucco a plaster used to cover exterior walls or decorate interior walls.

Tenant one who occupies property of another especially for rent.

Urban Relating to a city.

Barack Obama Timeline

1961 August 4 Barack Obama Jr. is born in Honolulu, Hawaii.

1967 Barry and his mother move to Indonesia with her new husband, Lolo.

1971 Barry moves back to the United States to live with his maternal grandparents in Honolulu again.

1979 Barry graduates high school in Hawaii and moves to Los Angeles to attend Occidental College. He meets a group of friends and starts to go by Barack.

1981 Barack transfers to Colombia University in New York to pursue a political science degree.

1985 Barack moves to Chicago to pursue a career in community organizing.

1987 Barack takes a trip to Kenya to help him understand his family and heritage.

1988 Barack is enrolled at Harvard Law School, where he becomes an editor of *The Harvard Law Review*.

1989 While working as a summer associate for Chicago law firm Sidley Austin, a twenty-seven-year-old Barack meets his future wife, Michelle Robinson.

1990 Barack is elected the president of *The Harvard Law Review* and becomes the first African American to hold this position. This gains him national media attention and a publishing contract for his first book.

1992 Michelle and Barack are married.

1993 Barack starts as a lecturer at the University of Chicago Law School and does this for 12 years.

1995 Barack's first book, *Dreams from My Father*, is published

World Timeline

1961 John F. Kennedy is inaugurated as President of the United States.

1967 The United States, Soviet Union, and Britain sign an Outer Space Treaty.

1974 President Richard Nixon resigns from office due to Watergate Scandal.

1979 A meltdown at a nuclear power plant on Three Mile Island, in Pennsylvania causes an above normal amount of radiation to be produced.

1981 Iran Hostage Crisis ends with a treaty signed by Iran and the United States.

1985 Microsoft Corporation releases Windows 1.0.

1987 The first US-Soviet treaty is signed regarding the destruction of nuclear weapons.

1988 Pan Am Flight 103 explodes, ending the company and killing 270 people.

1989 The Berlin Wall is torn down.

1990 East Germany holds its first free election since 1932.

1992 President Bush announces Operation Restore Hope to bring help to Somalia.

1994 Nelson Mandela becomes the first black president of South Africa.

1995 Yahoo is founded in Santa Clara, California.

Barack Obama Timeline (cont.)

1996 Barack is elected to the Illinois State Senate and stays for two terms.

1998 The Obama family's first daughter, Malia Ann, is born.

2000 Barack loses the democratic primary election for the Illinois seat in the House of Representatives.

2001 Daughter number two, Natasha (Sasha), is born.

2002 Barack is re-elected for a third term for the Illinois State Senate

2004 Elected to the United States Senate for the state of Illinois and resigns from the Illinois state senate.

2007 Barack announces his presidential candidacy in front of the Old State Capitol building in Springfield, Illinois.

2007 Delaware Senator, Joe Biden, is announced as Barack's running mate for the presidency.

2008 Barack is officially elected as the 44th President of the United States and becomes the first African American to hold this position.

2009 Appoints two women to serve on the Supreme Court including Sonia Sotomayor, the first Supreme Court Justice of Hispanic descent.

2012 Re-elected as the President of the United States

2013 Becomes the first president to call for full equality for gay Americans, and even mentions this is his second inarguable address.

2017 Barack's presidency officially ends.

World Timeline (cont.)

1996 The Taliban takes control of Jalalabad. The now control 70 percent of Afghanistan.

1998 *The Washington Post* reports the Clinton-Lewinsky affair.

2000 Vladimir Putin is elected president in Russia.

2001 World Trade Center destroyed by terrorists.

2003 Operation Red Dawn is conducted to capture Saddam Hussein and is successful.

2004 President Bush is re-elected.

2006 Facebook is accessible to anyone 13 years or older, not just college students.

2007 The Recession begins and becomes the largest economic crisis in the US since the Great Depression.

2008 The US elects its first black president.

2009 Twelve companies sign what was described as the largest solar energy project of all time.

2012 Obama is re-elected as president.

2013 Hillary Clinton resigns from her position as Secretary of State after suffering a concussion that caused her to stop travelling.

2017 Donald Trump is elected as the oldest president of the US.

Bibliography

Swaine, Michael, and Paul Freiberger, *Fire in the Valley: The Birth and Death of the Personal Computer*. The Pragmatic Bookshelf, 2014.

Jason Porterfield, *The Election of Barack Obama: Race and Politics in America* (In the News). Rosen Pub Group, 2010.

Jules Archer, *Winners and Losers: How Elections Work in America* (Jules Archer History for Young Readers). Sky Pony Press, 2016.

Sara Bullard, *Free At Last: A History of the Civil Rights Movement and Those Who Died in the Struggle*. Oxford University Press, 1993.

Henry Hampton, Steve Fayer, Sarah Flynn, *Voices of Freedom An Oral History of the Civil Rights Movement From the 1950s Through the 1980s*. Bantam Doubleday Dell, 1991.

Barack Obama, *The Audacity of Hope: Thoughts on Reclaiming the American Dream*. Broadway Books, 2007.

Barack Obama, *Dreams From My Father: A Story of Race and Inheritance*. Broadway Books, 2004.

Further Reading

Gormley, Beatrice. 2017. *Barak Obama: Our Forty-Fourth President*. Aladdin.

Obama, Barack. 2010. *Of Thee I Sing: A Letter to my Daughters*. New York: Random House Children's Books.

Souza, Pete. 2017. *Dream Big Dreams*. Little, Brown Books for Young Readers.

Obama, Michelle. 2018. *Becoming*. New York, New York: Crown Publishing Group.

Index

Index (cont.)

Index (cont.)

Index (cont.)

Index (cont.)

About the Authors

Paul Freiberger co-authored the best-selling *Fire in the Valley: The Making of the Personal Computer* (McGraw-Hill). He has produced reports for National Public Radio programs, including All Things Considered and Morning Edition.

Michael Swaine has been writing about technology full-time since he helped launch *Info World* in 1981. He co-wrote the seminal history of the personal computer, *Fire in the Valley*. He currently edits for *Pragmatic Programmers* and publishes a programming magazine called *PragPub*.

All About... Series

A series for inquisitive young readers

If you liked this book, you may also enjoy:

- All About Winston Churchill
- All About Roberto Clemente
- All About Frederick Douglass
- All About Amelia Earhart
- All About the Grand Canyon
- All About Benjamin Franklin
- All About Stephen Hawking
- All About Sir Edmund Hillary
- All About Helen Keller
- All About Martin Luther King, Jr.
- All About Julia Morgan
- All About Madam C. J. Walker
- All About Steve Wozniak
- All About Yellowstone
- All About the Great Lakes
- All About the Appalachian Trail
- All About Mohandas Gandhi

Visit brpressbooks.com for free teachers' guides, games, and puzzles.